MW00398252

I'M SORRY

Recovering

from the

Right to Choose

Carol Jackson

I'M SORRY: Recovering from the Right to Choose

Copyright © 2020 Carol J. Jackson

All rights reserved.

ISBN: 978-1-7923-5662-9

All Scripture quotations are taken from The Holy Bible, New International Version (NIV), copyright 1973, 1978, 1984 by International Bible Society. Used by permission of Zondervan. All rights reserved.

H.E.A.R.T. is a program of Pregnancy Decision Health Centers of Columbus, Ohio, Inc., a Heartbeat International Affiliate, 665 E. Dublin-Granville Road, Columbus, Ohio

For Mattie

For the glory of God

CONTENTS

1
I'm Sorry

Maybe no one has ever looked you directly in your eyes, then held you in their arms and said, "I'm sorry." It doesn't happen very often. So, I'm drawing you near right now to tell you, "I'm sorry."

I'm sorry someone told you that you had the right to choose. I'm sorry you wanted to believe it was true because you felt you had no other choice.

I'm sorry you felt you couldn't tell your parents that you were pregnant. If you did tell them, I'm sorry they kicked you out with no place to go. I'm sorry they forced you to have an abortion in order to remain their daughter. I'm sorry that your Dad has never looked at you the same since he learned his little princess was pregnant. I'm sorry they told you afterwards to get over it and move on with your life. I know it's not that easy. I'm sorry they convinced you a baby would ruin your life, when in the end, it seems it did anyway.

I'm sorry that the baby's father wasn't there to support you through your ordeal, or that he disappeared from your life soon after. I'm sorry he wasn't who you thought he was.

I'm sorry the nice people at the clinic lied right to your face and told you it was just fetal tissue, that it wasn't a baby yet, and that the 'tissue' wouldn't feel any pain. I'm sorry you so desperately wanted to believe them.

I'm sorry they didn't explain all your options so you could have made a better choice. I'm so sorry they took your money and then put you in the assembly line. I'm sorry if you felt like a piece of meat. I'm sorry you were surprised by the blood and the cramping afterwards.

I'm sorry for your tears. I'm sorry for the sounds, sights, and smells that you can't get out of your head. I'm sorry for the emptiness inside you. I'm sorry for the awful nightmares.

I'm sorry if you've never been able to conceive another child. I'm sorry if you feel you're being punished. I'm sorry if your other children have not been able to fill the void of the one you didn't bring to life. I'm sorry you keep wondering where your baby is now. I'm sorry you think the baby could never forgive you.

I'm sorry you were never able to share your problem with anyone else, that you had to keep your 'dirty little secret' to yourself all this time. I'm sorry that you saw judgment in the eyes of the one person you thought you could share your heart with. I'm truly sorry if that person was your pastor.

I'm so sorry you are still bound by chains of guilt and shame. I'm sorry you feel this is the one unforgivable sin. I'm sorry you're having relationship problems and that your life is falling apart, over and over again. I'm so sorry.

I can tell you "I'm sorry" because I've had years of experience feeling sorry for myself.

2
Betraying Myself

It was Friday, the 13th of March, when the supposedly impossible happened. I still recall every detail.

Not being the least bit superstitious, Friday the 13th was usually a lucky day for me. While others were actively looking for bad things to happen, I generally found the good things others missed, and that day was no exception. Having been 'lucky' for almost four years now, just using the rhythm method, and taking no other precautions, still I was surprised, albeit pleasantly, when I conceived my first child. I knew the moment of conception because I physically felt it. It can only describe it as a small twitch inside, but **I knew** instantly what had just happened. The doctor said it was impossible for me to have felt the conception, but **I knew** what happened that instant. **I knew** I was pregnant, and I wanted that baby. I think I fell in love with him that very day.

So, if I knew from the experience of having my first child that life began at conception, how did I later deceive myself into thinking that an abortion was an acceptable form of birth control? I knew better. And therein lies the betrayal.

A woman so betrays her own self when she kills her unborn child that she's never the same again. I know I never was.

So, you've had an abortion, and you feel betrayed. Your pregnant body has been betrayed, and now your mind and soul feel the pain as well. You are emotionally traumatized. You violated the law of nature in taking a life, rather than being the life-bearer. A child is dead – your child.

It's perfectly legal, so no one is coming to arrest you to make you pay for what you did. But surely, someone should have to pay for this, so you take on that duty yourself and subconsciously start to punish yourself. It gets ugly.

Abortion is such an ugly topic for a book – hard to hear, but it needs to be heard. One of the devil's best ploys is to keep post-abortive women locked in shame and silence, and everyone else leery of speaking up for fear of being politically incorrect. But healing starts with breaking the silence. This book is about healing from the right to choose.

I want to make certain that you understand up front that I'm not trying to rationalize or justify my abortion. I'm not making any excuses for what I did. I take full responsibility for the death of my unborn child and I realize I will have to deal with the consequences of my actions for the rest of my life. But I do know that I am deeply loved and that I am forgiven. You can know that, too.

Sometimes it helps just knowing you're not alone, that your feelings aren't abnormal, that others have walked in your steps and not only survived, but thrived. Sometimes hearing someone else's story helps. God has blessed me with the ability to be transparent about my abortion and to minister to post-abortive women with the authority of one totally redeemed! So, I share my personal story of recovering from the right to choose in the hope of bringing healing to your life.

3

Innocence Lost

My favorite picture of me was taken when I was about three. If I do say so myself, I was an adorable little girl with my blond curls, and very sweet and innocent looking. I don't actually remember being three, just seeing the picture, but I always wanted to be that sweet, innocent little girl. My earliest memory is actually from kindergarten. Our classroom was a big round room with lots of windows; it's where we learned stuff, took naps on mats, wore pretty dresses, and got to play duck, duck, goose. I loved it!

By the time I had my school picture taken in second grade, my whole appearance had changed. I had become what my father called sullen. He also labeled me emotionally unstable. Apparently, you become sullen and emotionally unstable when you feel unloved. During my second grade year, my favorite teacher, Mrs. Thiel, called my parents to let them know I had shared with the class that my parents didn't love me and, in my seven-year-old mind, I must have been adopted. I recall being chastised for revealing my feelings; after all, what would the neighbors think if they knew I felt unloved? I got scolded for potentially embarrassing my father. It was explained to me that an adopted child had been chosen and therefore, *was* loved. But since it was also made clear to me that I was definitely not adopted, my mind reasoned that I was correct in my thinking that they were just stuck with me, and that I was, in fact, not loved. That wasn't their intent, but that's what I took from the talk. There was no attempt to understand why I felt unloved.

I think it all stemmed from the fact that in first grade I was molested by a friend's older brother. To this day, I can't tell you exactly what went on, but somehow at six, I knew something wasn't quite right. I didn't know enough to tell my parents what had happened. After all, I was only six. But I started wetting the bed, and I got punished for it. My parents didn't know enough back then to recognize my behavior as a sign of child molestation. I couldn't play outside after 4:00 o'clock and wasn't allowed anything to drink after dinner. It obviously made me "sullen and emotionally unstable."

I thought whatever Martha's older brother did to me must have been my fault and that there was something seriously wrong with me. I was flawed. That's probably why my parents couldn't love me like my friend Vicky's parents obviously loved her. I loved going to Vicky's house and being around her family. I can still remember the smell of cinnamon bread that emanated from their kitchen, amongst the sounds of laughter. I always felt safe there, and loved, even if I was just Vicky's friend.

I spent the rest of my childhood living up to my father's expectations. It was hard work being sullen and emotionally unstable! I never told my big sis, Sheri, either because I didn't want her to not love me. She was my first friend, and she's still my favorite friend. The only other person who I knew loved me was my baby sister, Janet, who adored me and Sheri and called us 'the dolls' since she couldn't say 'girls'. I'm still Janet's favorite sister. I'm certain now that my mother loved me too, but she wasn't overly demonstrative in her affections.

Although my brain has since blocked the memories of what happened to me in that basement, I must have remembered back then because it awakened something in me that I was way too young to comprehend, which could have made me an unknowing target for other predators. Being awakened to sexuality at age six is a very confusing experience. It could even make you sullen or emotionally unstable. As I was growing up, I knew 'stuff' that I had no earthly idea how I knew, and yet I was also naïve.

I started smoking and drinking when I was thirteen. I guess my dad didn't notice because he smoked and drank. (I wonder what the neighbors thought about the times he came home drunk? I know it embarrassed me!) He was a real gem of a Dad. He used to take his belt to us, all the while screaming, "Don't you cry!" but we knew he wouldn't stop until we did. What a dilemma for little girls. I think he just had a mean streak. He would find out what we wanted most for Christmas, and that would be the one gift our Mom wasn't allowed to buy us. Supposedly, he didn't want to spoil us.

I narrowly escaped a gang rape at a drunken party at age thirteen. Shortly thereafter the suicidal thoughts, which plagued me most of my early life, began. I had my Dad's gun in my hand, but then was startled out of my intent to end it all when the phone rang. I think now that it was God's way of intervening way back then.

My least favorite photo of me was taken about that time in middle school. My hair was curled but not combed out much and I looked ridiculous. I've wondered since how my family could have let me out of the house looking like a freak. But that was when my father had lost his job and started drinking more, and my mother had gone to work, probably to keep the family afloat financially. That's also when my older sister Sheri met her future husband and was totally distracted with him. There was no one to look after me, or so it seemed, and I felt all alone.

When I lost my virginity at fourteen to a predator at high school, it was hurtful, not the pleasurable experience I was anticipating. I've learned since that many post-abortive women were molested as children. It makes sense that once you've been devalued yourself, it makes it easier to devalue your unborn child.

Another wound that festered with me for years was my father's attempt at humor. He repeatedly told me I was pretty – pretty ugly and pretty apt to stay that way. What he thought was funny cursed me for decades. I was a pretty girl, but I only saw the ugliness in my soul.

By the time I was eighteen, I was sick with ulcerative colitis and ended up on tranquilizers just to function. I drank to escape who I was and the stress of my home life, and I was looking for love in all the wrong places, as they say. A sullen and emotionally unstable child had morphed into a very angry, empty young woman.

4
The Wrong Choice

In 1970 I married my high school sweetheart since we were pregnant, and seven months later I gave birth to an adorable little boy. I had a normal delivery, no complications, brought him home on Christmas morning, put him under the Christmas tree, and took his picture. He was my gift from God and I delighted in him. I had been totally in love with my son for nine months already, since the moment of conception. Finally, someone who would love me!

Sometime in the next year and a half, I found myself pregnant again. Out of pure selfishness, I did not want another child because I did not want to experience labor pains again. Sometime in late 1971 or early 1972, before Roe v. Wade, when it was only legal in New York and California, my husband and I traveled to New York City and aborted our second child. Problem solved, or so I thought.

That day had to be absolutely the worst day of my life. Funny thing, though, I don't know when it was. I don't know the day of the week, although I'd guess a Friday or a Saturday. I can't tell you what season of the year it was – no clue. I'm not even sure what year it was. And I don't know where I was, other than somewhere in New York City. I do remember it was early morning.

So how could I not know all of these details about what was the darkest day of my life? How could I have completely blocked out everything but early morning in New York City? I don't know the name of the doctor, or the clinic. Maybe I don't want to know. Maybe it's a blessing that I don't remember anything else. Maybe my mind was protecting me from the horror of what I did to my unborn child that day. I now know that blocking memories of an abortion is a very common survival technique with post-abortive women.

I don't recall the procedure at all. I only remember flying home and not feeling so swell. I didn't realize it then, but it was the worst day of my life. My husband and I never spoke of it again, and I never told anyone what I had done.

At some point, I decided I didn't want my son to be an only child, and I chose to get pregnant again. When my son was 3-1/2 years old, I was surprised at delivery with twin girls, delivered Caesarean section. For a while I thought God was punishing me for aborting my second child. I thought he had decided that I was having three children, so here was the aborted baby back again. It wasn't until the girls were toddlers that I began to see them as a blessing, not a punishment. I took good care of them and loved them, but I never really allowed myself to enjoy the girls as babies like I had with their brother. I've also realized that over the years I have avoided holding babies, and still generally don't, except for my own grandchildren. I had an especially difficult time holding my first grandson who was born at twenty-six weeks, weighing under two pounds.

I really did have a good life back then. I had a good-looking husband who was a good provider, a dear son and darling twin daughters, a nice home in a good neighborhood, a decent job, lots of friends. But I wasn't happy living the good life.

5

A Hot Mess

The next three decades were rough ones. I spent a great deal of time in self-destructive behaviors, subconsciously punishing myself. I sabotaged my marriage. I loved my husband and wanted to try counseling to save our marriage, but we went to one session and he said he was done. There was nothing wrong with our marriage as far as he was concerned. But I was still struggling. I think the current terminology is a hot mess. I didn't even know at that time how much baggage I was hauling around from my childhood.

I think the final nail in the coffin of our marriage was when he told me he owned me. "I own you" triggered something in me - owned, unloved, used, ugly. My survival instincts kicked in, and I had to prove it wasn't true. I moved him into the category of men who use women and I couldn't move beyond it. Looking back now, I think if he hadn't remarried four months later, and if I had gotten some much-needed counseling, we might have been able to reconcile down the road.

Subconsciously I blamed my husband for not standing up to me and saying no to the abortion, because I wasn't able then to accept responsibility for my own actions.

Women who abort their babies instinctively know that what they've done is wrong. We're supposed to be the life-bearers, not the life-takers. When my husband and I got divorced on our ninth anniversary, my life further unraveled, and I sank into depression.

I further compounded my mess a couple years later when I agreed to let my son live with his father. With the attitude of distrust I had developed towards men, I didn't think I could teach him how to be a good man. It broke my heart to let him go, but I did what I thought was best for him at the time, even though it worsened my depression. Today he is a fine husband, father and provider for his family, so at least that turned out right.

An incident that occurred with my girls when they were in middle school had a big impact on my thinking over the years. I was driving them and their friends somewhere, and in conversation I made the statement that I knew I had taught my daughters three important life concepts. I expected them to say: God loves me, my Mother loves me, and blood is thicker than water (i.e. family should always stick together). What came out of their mouths, in unison no less, was: God loves me, my Mother loves me, and all men are bastards! I believed that, but I didn't realize I had infected my daughters with my cynicism. I have had to work extremely hard over the years to overcome my dislike of men.

During this season of my life, I led a secret promiscuous lifestyle and numbed myself with food, alcohol and sometimes drugs, which is very typical of post-abortive women. My life looked good on the outside, but I hated myself. Had I not feared the devastating effects on my three living children, I would have committed suicide. I spent hours planning how to do it and trying to work up the courage. I did make one half-hearted attempt, but at the last minute I saw the truck driver's panicked face, because he didn't want to die with me, and I pulled back into my own lane.

I think that God has protected me by blocking the memories of the abortion. I have asked God to restore my memories if it would help me to help other women, but I still don't remember anything. Some women recall every detail, so I'm considering this a blessing. I know that if I remembered going through some of the horrific abortion experiences that women I've counseled have shared with me, I would have found a way to take my own life. Now I can see that it was God's grace that saved me – because he knew he could use me now to help other women.

At the same time as my life was unraveling behind the scenes, I was also active in my church, having grown up in the church. I taught Sunday school, went on a mission trip, and worked on the Billy Graham Crusade team when he came to Cleveland. I had a responsible job, moving up from an administration position into management. I got elected to the local school board. I had three great kids, and although I was a bit over-protective, I was a good mom. All three of my children have become responsible adults, with good jobs, wonderful mates, and well-behaved children. They continue to bring incredible joy to my life.

Seemingly overnight, I hit my forties – ready for 'life to begin,' as they say. I had fearfully struggled through several major surgeries, miraculously surviving melanoma. Both of my parents had passed on, my older sister and her family lived halfway across the country, and my younger sister was permanently in nursing care with brain damage from a car accident. I was twice divorced by then. So, when my kids went off to college, I found myself all alone **again**.

After weeks wallowing in my initial panic, I eventually realized God hadn't brought me this far to abandon me now. There was just the ever so slight glimmer of contentment growing in me. God had brought me through so much already; perhaps He had a plan to heal my life after all.

6
Healing My H.E.A.R.T.

Because I had been so successful in blocking memories of the abortion, I never made any connection with the mess my life was, until I turned on the car radio one day. I was driving and listening to Dr. James Dobson of Focus on the Family interview some woman about post-abortion syndrome; I had never heard of it. By the time she got done explaining it, I was crying so hard I had to pull off the road. God convicted me right then and there. I had all but one of the symptoms.

A friend at my church helped me get connected to the Cleveland Pregnancy Center and into a H.E.A.R.T. group. H.E.A.R.T. stands for Healing the Effects of Abortion Related Trauma. H.E.A.R.T. is a strictly confidential, Christ-centered, Bible-based, seven-week workshop that takes women (or men) through the steps for healing: acknowledging the abortion for what it was, forgiving others involved in the abortion, seeking and receiving forgiveness from God, the child and yourself, grieving the loss of the child, and memorializing your baby. It is a gut-wrenching experience, but Jesus uses it to bring healing.

The H.E.A.R.T. program is facilitated by other post-abortive women who know exactly how you feel, because they've been there themselves; consequently, there's no judgment. We share our personal stories and ask the participants to do the same; sometimes it's the first time a woman has ever told anyone about her abortion.

We talk about the anger, and guilt, and shame, and grief, and the coping mechanisms we used to try to survive. We forgive others who were involved in our abortion.

We talk about who God is — about his character, and his loving kindness, and his mercy. And we remind the ladies that when they ask Him for forgiveness, that isn't when He first found out about their abortion. God knew before you were born that you'd have an abortion, and He still created you!

We talk about the babies, too, and honor them.

Each week builds on the week before, so when we get to the end of the workshop and ask the ladies to accept God's forgiveness by forgiving themselves, the real healing begins.

Previously, I had allowed God to forgive me for all of my many sins – except the abortion. Even though I had Romans 8:1 (Therefore, there is now no condemnation for those who are in Christ Jesus.) highlighted in my Bible, I was still living under condemnation. Like so many post-abortive women, I didn't feel I deserved to be forgiven for what I'd done, so I refused to forgive myself or accept God's forgiveness. Someone pointed out to me that refusing forgiveness was actually ascribing more power to my sin than to the blood of Jesus, which was sin itself.

One aspect of the healing process that impacted me tremendously was dealing with my grief. Apparently, a great deal of what I had been experiencing as guilt and shame was actually unreleased grief. Society expects you to grieve the loss of your parents, a sibling, your spouse, a child, even your friends, but it doesn't recognize or understand your need to grieve a fetus you chose to abort. I had unknowingly been struggling for decades with the earlier stages of grief, but I had never come to the last stage of acceptance. Being granted permission to grieve the loss of my son was life-giving.

One particular night at 3 AM, during the seven-week program, when I was totally broken and finally at the end of my own ugliness and pride, I surrendered my life to Jesus and accepted the forgiveness he provided on the cross. I told him he could do with me as he pleased, even if he struck me dead on the spot. Soon thereafter I experienced the Holy Spirit in my life for the first time. I had a lot of head knowledge about God, but discovering that God is really REAL, and that you can experience the presence of the Holy Spirit in your life right now radically transformed my faith. Who would have imagined that the Creator of the universe would take the time to actually speak to someone like me?

If you had told me prior to the H.E.A.R.T. program that God was going to call me to get up one Sunday morning and admit my abortion to my own church family, and then go to other churches and tell them about it, I would have said, "not in this life." But God did call me to share the hope I have with others who need healing. I have such a peace and calm about sharing that it has to be from him, and he keeps opening up opportunities for me to share. This book was his idea, too. He's actually woken me up in the early morning on numerous occasions, giving me the content, as I've been ready to receive it. He is so faithful.

God's hand has been evident in this whole process. For example, during the H.E.A.R.T. workshop I named my unborn child Matthew Zachary. After the workshop I chose to sponsor a child through the Christian Children's Fund. I requested a little boy anywhere in the world and was given a three-year-old in Brazil. Imagine my joy when I learned his name was

Mateus, which in Brazilian Portuguese means Matthew. Two years later his brother arrived. I don't know exactly what Zaquelle means, but to me it's Zachary. God is so good to connect me with these two little boys to help them live a better life.

Another of the ways I chose to honor my unborn child was to purchase a plaque at the National Memorial for the Unborn in Chattanooga, Tennessee. I visited there a few years back, and it was such a moving experience. I highly recommend it.

7
Freedom!

A year or so after I went through the program, I started volunteering at the Cleveland Pregnancy Center, facilitating the H.E.A.R.T. groups. For over a decade, I helped numerous wounded women find healing through Jesus. After a couple of years, I started worrying because I wasn't feeling bad about my abortion anymore, and I wondered if I had done so many groups that my heart had hardened. Then I came across some material in a Beth Moore Bible study about total redemption, and it hit me like a ton of bricks! John 8:36 says, "If the Son shall set you free, you shall be free indeed!" That means one hundred percent free! – not fifty percent, or even ninety-five percent, but completely free - 100%!!!

That's what God has done for me. He has set me completely free from condemnation. Free to love him with my whole heart – with all my heart, soul, strength and mind! I don't have to be afraid to come to him with my other sins because he's already forgiven me for more than I could ever have dared hope. I'M FREE!

I didn't think that was possible, even after I knew I was forgiven. But I am TOTALLY FREE!

8
Perfect Peace

A few years back I was invited to speak at my friend's church. For his sermon that day, the pastor interviewed my friend Sue and I about the healing God had brought to our lives after Sue's miscarriage and my abortion. While preparing for the service, the pastor learned that we wrote letters in the H.E.A.R.T. program and asked if I would be willing to read my letter to my unborn child. Since I had never read the letter before without breaking down into tears, and since the focus of our conversation was on the healing we had received, I didn't see how my weeping would be of help to anyone, so I declined. He asked me to pray about it, so I did, but with no positive results. When the day came, I did, however, bring the letter with me to the church service, but with no intentions of reading it.

The service began with some worship songs. While worshipping I clearly heard the Lord say, "I will hold you in perfect peace." My mouth literally dropped open because I knew He wanted me to read my letter! He said again, "I will hold you in perfect peace." My heart was in turmoil. I so wanted to be obedient, but I also didn't want to fall apart in front of hundreds of people who expected to hear how 100% free I was.

When we got to that time in the service, and the pastor asked me about the letters we wrote in the H.E.A.R.T. program, God was faithful to hold me in perfect peace while I read:

My dear son,

I am so sorry that I took your precious life from you. I had no right to make such a choice. There are no excuses or extenuating circumstances for what I did, other than my own selfishness. I'm sorry also that I denied your existence for so long - 28 years - but my guilt and shame for my heinous act would not allow me to acknowledge you. I still find it hard to believe that I ended your precious life.

I would gladly give my own life now to restore yours, but that is not possible.

I have asked God for His forgiveness and I believe now He

has forgiven me. I can only pray you can forgive me someday when we meet in Heaven.

You have an older brother, and twin sisters, who are about two years younger. I know you and your big brother would have been close since you're only about a year and a half younger. They all know about you now, and I know they all wish, as I do, that you were here sharing this earthly life with us; I feel certain your Dad would love to know his second son as well.

I have finally chosen a name for you after 28 years of secrecy: Matthew (which means gift of God) Zachary (meaning God has remembered). I know God remembered you these 28 years when I failed to acknowledge His gift to me.

I'm choosing to celebrate your expected date of birth as May 9, 1972, which was your father's and my second wedding anniversary.

You are being dedicated to the Lord on Saturday, January 6, 2001, and you will be honored at the National Memorial for the Unborn. From now on I will no longer grieve for you, my lost son, but will celebrate you, for I know you have always lived on in Heaven in the arms of Jesus.

How I long to know you, to hold you, to love you as I should have, my son. Someday I know I will. Until that day, Mattie, please know that I do love you with all my heart.

Mom

Sue told me later you could have heard a pin drop in that room. I was unaware. I was in perfect peace.

9

The Woman at the Well

John 4:5-29 relays the well-known story of the Samaritan woman that Jesus encounters at the well. Here's the narrative:

So, he came to a town in Samaria called Sychar, near the plot of ground Jacob had given to this son Joseph. Jacob's well was there, and Jesus, tired as he was from the journey, sat down by the well. It was about the sixth hour.

When a Samaritan woman came to draw water, Jesus said to her, "Will you give me a drink?" (His disciples had gone into town to buy food.)

The Samaritan woman said to him, "You are a Jew and I am a Samaritan woman. How can you ask me for a drink?" (For Jews do not associate with Samaritans.)

Jesus answered her, "If you knew the gift of God and who it is that asks you for a drink, you would have asked him and he would have given you living water."

"Sir," the woman said, "you have nothing to draw with and the well is deep. Where can you get this living water? Are you greater than our father Jacob, who gave us the well and drank from it himself, as did also his sons and his flocks and herds?"

Jesus answered, "Everyone who drinks this water will be thirsty again, but whoever drinks the water I give him will never thirst. Indeed, the water I give him will become in him a spring of water welling up to eternal life."

The woman said to him, "Sir, give me this water so that I don't get thirsty and have to keep coming here to draw water."

He told her, "Go, call your husband and come back."

"I have no husband," she replied.

Jesus said to her, "You are right when you say you have no husband. The fact is, you have had five husbands, and the man you now have is not your husband. What you have said is quite true."

"Sir," the woman said, "I can see that you are a prophet. Our fathers worshipped on this mountain, but you Jews claim that the place we must worship is in Jerusalem."

Jesus declared, "Believe me, woman, a time is coming when you will worship the Father neither on this mountain nor in Jerusalem. You Samaritans worship what you do not know; we worship what we do know, for salvation is from the Jews. Yet a time is coming and has now come when the true worshipers will worship the Father in spirit and truth, for they are the kind of worshipers the Father seeks. God is spirit, and his worshipers must worship in spirit and in truth."

The woman said, "I know that Messiah (called Christ) is coming. When he comes, he will explain everything to us."

The Jesus declared, "I who speak to you am he."

Just then his disciples returned and were surprised to find him talking with a woman. But no one asked, "What do you want?" or "Why are you talking with her?"

Then, leaving her water jar, the woman went back to the town and said to the people, "Come, see a man who told me everything I ever did. Could this be the Christ?"

In the past, I could easily relate to the Samaritan woman, the outsider who was suspicious of men's motives, having had five husbands, working on another. (I'm only on number three.) The one whose innocence was long gone. She's the one who was always alone. The one who was empty, always needing 'something.' The woman with head knowledge about God, but never having encountered him in her heart. The woman who had to be tough to survive, but who desperately wanted to be loved and cherished.

There's no specific mention in the Bible of what happened to this woman after her personal encounter with Jesus at the well, only that Jesus stayed in Sychar two days at the townspeople's request, and that many became believers. I like to think that, with God's help, she turned her life around, became one of those true worshipers Jesus talked about. In my version of her story, she knows she's forgiven, she doesn't feel alone anymore, and she knows she's found what she's always been longing for – Jesus Himself. I think she's free – like me!

Maybe you've also been the woman at the well, longing to trade your self-proclaimed tramp stamp for something else – someone else. Wouldn't you like to meet Jesus and let him change your middle name from 'shame' to something lovely like grace, or joy, or beloved, perhaps? Wouldn't you like to be truly free?

10
Beloved

I have another favorite picture. My third marriage has lasted, unlike the other two, and my husband Bill and I renewed our wedding vows on our sixteenth wedding anniversary. We had a real wedding that time. I wore a long ivory dress and my husband looked so handsome in his Marine Corps dress blues. I walked down the aisle to the words of Brent Helming's worship song, "Your Beloved":

I am your beloved, your
creation,
and you love me as I am.
You have called me chosen for
your kingdom.
Unashamed to call me your own.
I am your beloved.

It was so special.

We worshipped, then renewed
our vows before God and our
church family, and afterwards
celebrated with family and friends at
a lovely luncheon reception. It was
one of the best days of my life, and
I felt truly beautiful for the first time
in my life. I felt beautiful, not only
as Bill's earthly bride, but it was also
like a little taste of being the Bride
of Christ (Revelation 19:7-8).
Beautiful, smiling, clean, joyful,
whole, content, at peace – thank
you, Jesus!

Unfortunately, my dear husband has developed memory loss. Alzheimer's is such a nasty disease, but we are dealing with it, and after twenty-five years together, we still have a wonderful life. I just have to remember things for both of us. That means I have to stay on top of everything, which can be difficult at times; I guess it's good that I'm super-organized.

They say God uses everything for good, and I can see that God has even used Bill's unfortunate memory loss to help heal me. Bill tells me numerous times during each day how much he loves me, and how beautiful he thinks I am. (I tell him he needs to get his eyes checked!) The effect has been that I have stopped seeing myself as 'pretty ugly and pretty apt to stay that way' and that I have allowed myself to grasp hold of unconditional love. I know I am loved completely – by Bill, but also by my Heavenly Father. It's a blessing I never expected to come from an illness.

Another blessing has been realized recently as well. When growing up I always said I wanted to have six kids. (I temporarily recanted that goal through gritted teeth during labor pains of my first childbirth, as I recall.) I think I related lots of kids to a happy home life, like my friend Vicky had. There were lots of kids, and Auntie Bev, and loving parents at Vicky's, besides the cinnamon bread, and I wanted that. Recently God showed me that He did bless me with the six children I always wanted. My firstborn son, my twin daughters, and Mattie in heaven makes four. Plus, my hubby has two wonderful children, a son and a daughter who

I have come to love as my very own. That makes six. You have given me the desire of my heart, Father (Psalm 37:4).

I have one final picture that I treasure above all others. Completely out of the blue, on September 21, 2018, God so graciously showed me a vision of my unborn son. Mattie is an adorable little boy with blond curls and beautiful blue eyes. He looks a lot like his brother. His eyes were wide with wonder and delight, like mine, because he was seeing me, his mother, for the first time, too, at that same moment. There was such love in our eyes! You could never erase that picture from my mind. I look forward to seeing him again in Heaven.

11
The Lies

I used to wonder how I could have done such a wicked thing. When God gave us the gift of free will, that included the ability to make choices, both good and bad. When we make a really bad choice, we also get to suffer the consequences. My choosing to abort was one of those really bad choices. But even here, what Satan meant for evil, God can use for good (Genesis 50:20). After a great deal of questioning, arguing, pondering, and the like, I've come to the realization that if I hadn't gone through so many years of self-condemnation, self-loathing, guilt, and shame, rightfully suffering the consequences of my right to choose, I may never have come to the end of my miserable self and totally surrendered my life to Christ. That was the ultimate purpose in his allowing my abortion.

God also knew that I would be able to speak freely, not only about what I've done, but what God has done to restore my life. He knew he could use me to help other post-abortive women find the healing I've found.

If you've made a bad choice about abortion, (or anything else for which you've condemned yourself, for that matter), I John 1:9 promises, "If we confess our sins, he is faithful and just and will forgive our sins and cleanse us from all unrighteousness." And that includes abortion. There is NO sin so big that Christ's blood on the cross hasn't already covered it.

I'm sorry I didn't know the truth back then. I'd like to think my life would have been so much different, and someone else would be writing this book. But there's no way to change the past. It is what it is. So, since it is me writing, there are a few more things I would like to address.

There are so many untruths around the whole abortion topic. The whole industry has been based on deceit, right from the beginning. For example, did you know that Norma McCorvey, Jane Roe of Roe v. Wade, never did have an abortion? As soon as her feminist attorneys got her signature to get the test case on the court docket, they stopped returning her phone calls. She had her baby and put her up for adoption. Years later, she gave her heart to Jesus when Operation Rescue moved in next door to the abortion clinic where she worked and wouldn't give up on her. Now she heads up a pro-life ministry, and she has a relationship with the daughter she didn't abort. Her book, <u>Won by Love</u>, is an excellent read.

Abortion is certainly not about a women's right to choose, as our culture would like you to believe. If it were, the clinics would want you to know ALL the facts so you could make an informed decision. They would want to make sure no young woman was ever pressured to abort against her will, giving up her right to choose life, because someone else wanted to exercise their "right to choose" for her. Certainly, they would want an underage girl's parents, the ones who love her most, to be informed in advance of the surgical procedure, just in case something went wrong (which it does more often than you might think).

If they wanted you to know all the facts so you could make the best decision, they would want you to see an ultrasound of your child, to know how far the baby has developed so you could understand what aborting might do to the baby. However, they know women who see an ultrasound first are 93% more likely to choose life. They know that if you hear a heartbeat (21 days), or see that the baby responds to touch at 8 weeks, or see that your nine-week-old baby is sucking its thumb, that you might change your mind about having the 'tissue' scraped or suctioned and dismembered from your womb. They would tell you exactly how the surgical procedure is performed, what happens to the fetus (Latin for 'young one') during and after the procedure. They would also tell you what happens to the body parts afterwards: do they sell them to a research lab or just, literally, toss them in the trash?

And because they are all about your rights, of course they would tell you about the now well-documented possible post-abortion after-effects you might experience – the shame, guilt, anxiety, depression, suicidal thoughts, the grief! Who wouldn't sign up for that? They will probably not mention that the relationship you're trying to salvage by aborting the baby is highly unlikely to survive. When the baby daddy is pushing for the abortion, it almost always ends up dividing the couple, no matter how much they are in love at the moment of the decision.

So, if abortion is not about a woman's right to choose, then what's the deal? Its original roots are in racism and in eliminating all of the physically and mentally handicapped from society, but it has evolved and now the abortion industry is all about money – BIG MONEY. Don't let anyone tell you otherwise. If they tell you the truth about abortion, you're likely to choose life for your baby, and they won't make any money! Isn't there a Scripture verse about the love of money being the root of all evil? (I Timothy 6:10)

12
The Truth

I'm thankful that God has revealed His truth to me, and that The Truth (Jesus) has set me free from my right to choose (John 14:6).

God wants you to know the truth, too.

God wants to look directly into your eyes, hold you in His arms and say "I'm sorry." He wants to draw you near right now. Will you listen to Him?

Hear him say, "I'm sorry someone told you that you had the right to choose, and that you so desperately wanted it to be true. That was never your right, my child. When I created you in my image (Genesis 1:26), the gift of choice was an inherent part of your free will, but I also set parameters for you for right living when I gave you the commandments not to steal, not to commit adultery, not to kill, not to lie or covet (Exodus 20:1-17). Deuteronomy 30:19 is very clear in telling you to choose life, so that you and your children may live... I'm sorry you chose poorly.

I'm sorry that you live in a world that values your right to control your body over the truth. My Word warns you not to lean on your own understanding (Proverbs 3:5) and that there is a way that seems right to a person, but eventually it ends in death (Proverbs 16:25). My ways are not your ways (Isaiah 55:9).

I'm sorry your parents failed you, and that the one you thought you loved abandoned you. Come to me, get to know me, and you will see that I am the faithful one (Psalm 36:5). I will never leave you or forsake you (Deuteronomy 31:6).

I'm sorry you were told lies about the procedure, about the baby within your womb, and that you felt you needed to believe them. The devil is the father of all lies (John 8:44), and he has a stronghold in the pro-abortion camp. I'm so sorry for the horrors you experienced. I never wanted that for you. I can see that you are brokenhearted over your decision, and I want to heal your wounds. (Psalm 147:3).

I'm sorry that you feel as if you are Rachel weeping for her children and refusing to be comforted because they are no more (Matthew 2:18), and that you feel you are being punished. If you are honest with yourself, you will see that you are the one doing the punishing. I don't work that way. I am a merciful God, gracious and compassionate (2 Chronicles 30:9).

I'm sorry you struggle with thoughts of your little one, wondering if he could ever forgive you for what you did. I have known your child from conception (Psalm 139:13-16) and have loved and cared for him with an everlasting love (Jeremiah 31:3). Since there are no tears in heaven, nor death, nor mourning, nor crying, nor pain (Revelation 21:4), there is no reason to believe your child lives in unforgiveness. That is another of

68

the devil's lies, intended to keep you at arm's length from Me.

I'm sorry for the judgment you've felt. Unfortunately, those who judge will eventually be judged by that same measure (Matthew 7:2). I am the only righteous judge (Psalm 98:8-9), and I have the authority to forgive your sins and remove them from your life (Psalm 103:12). I long to do that for you, dear one.

I'm sorry you've gotten it in your head that abortion is the one unforgiveable sin. 1 John 1:9 promises, "If we confess our sins, he is faithful and just and will forgive us our sins and purify us from **all** unrighteousness." That little word 'all' includes abortion, too. Don't let society, or even the church, tell you otherwise. If I forgave those who crucified me while I was still hanging on the cross

(Luke 23:34), surely, I will forgive you for your sin of abortion.

I'm sorry you think no one understands your pain. More than anyone else, I do know your pain. When I paid the debt for all of the world's sin on the cross, (I John 2:2) I also bore all the pain, all of the shame, all of the torment (1 Corinthians 6:20). I know your pain, and much more.

I'm sorry you are struggling under the chains of guilt and shame. I long for you to be free (2 Corinthians 3:17). If you will let me, I can and will set you free (John 8:36). I have provided a way for you, but you have to literally be willing to walk out of the self-imposed prison cell you've been sitting in for so long. Your debt has already been paid in full. You're free to go. Don't let pride keep you there.

Invitation to Freedom

It's true. I bore your pain; I paid your debt. But that was just the beginning, dear one. I defeated sin and death by my resurrection from the grave, and I am more alive than you can even imagine! I died and rose again to redeem my creation from its fallen state, to redeem **you** from your mistakes and poor choices.

I'm not inviting you to a religion or a set of standards, or some rituals

I need you to perform. I'm inviting you to a personal relationship with me, your Savior. I want to open for you, like I did for Carol, my 'song of joy,' the doors to eternity, a spiritual realm you never knew existed.

It's really very simple. Let me draw you near, hold you close. Tell me that you're sorry for what you have done, that you know that you need me as your Savior. Say, "I want you in my life. Please forgive me, Jesus." Invite me into your heart to live and reign, and to fill you with My presence. Let me transform your life and make you into a new creation. I will set you free! Please come. I'm waiting with open arms.

Jesus

Jesus straightened up and asked
her,

"Woman, where are they? Has no
one condemned you?"

"No one, sir," she said.

"Then neither do I condemn you,"
Jesus declared.

"Go now and leave your life of
sin."

John 8:10-11

Scripture References

Revelation 19:7-8 Let us rejoice and be glad and give him glory! For the wedding of the Lamb has come, and his bride has made herself ready. Fine linen, bright and clean, was given her to wear.

Psalm 37:4 Delight yourself in the Lord and he will give you the desires of your heart.

Genesis 50:20 You intended to harm me, but God intended it for good to accomplish what is now being done, the saving of many lives.

I Timothy 6:10 For the love of money is a root of all kinds of evil. Some people, eager for money, have wandered from the faith and pierced themselves with many griefs.

John 14:6   Jesus answered, "I am the way and the truth and the life. No one comes to the Father except through me."

Genesis 1:26   Then God said, "Let us make man in our image, in our likeness, and let them rule over the fish of the sea and the birds of the air, and over all the creatures that move along the ground."

Exodus 20:1-17   And God spoke all these words:

I am the Lord your God, who brought you out of Egypt, out of the land of slavery.

You shall have no other gods before me.

You shall not make for yourself an idol in the form of anything in heaven above or on the earth beneath or in the waters below. You shall not bow down to them or worship them; for I, the

Lord your God, am a jealous God, punishing the children for the sin of the fathers to the third and fourth generation of those who hate me, but showing love to a thousand generations of those who love me and keep my commandments.

You shall not misuse the name of the Lord your God, for the Lord will not hold anyone guiltless who misuses his name.

Remember the Sabbath day by keeping it holy. Six days shall you labor and do all your work, but the seventh day is a Sabbath to the Lord your God. On it you shall not do any work, neither you, nor your son or daughter, nor your manservant or maidservant, nor your animals, nor the alien within your gates. For in six days the Lord made the heavens and the earth, the sea, and all that is in them, but he rested on the seventh day. Therefore the Lord blessed the Sabbath day and made it holy.

Honor your father and your mother so that you may live long in the land the Lord your God is giving you.

You shall not murder.

You shall not commit adultery.

You shall not steal.

You shall not give false testimony against your neighbor.

You shall not covet your neighbor's house. You shall not covet your neighbor's wife, or his manservant or maidservant, his ox or donkey, or anything that belongs to your neighbor.

Deuteronomy 30:19 This day I call heaven and earth as witnesses against you that I have set before you lie and death, blessings and curses. Now choose life, so that you and your children may live.

Proverbs 3:5   Trust in the Lord with all your heart and lean not on your own understanding.

Proverbs 16:25   There is a way that seems right to a man, but in the end, it leads to death.

Isaiah 55:9   As the heavens are higher than the earth, so are my ways higher than your ways and my thoughts than your thoughts.

Psalm 36:5   Your love, O Lord, reaches to the heavens, your faithfulness to the skies.

Deuteronomy 31:6   Be strong and courageous. Do not be afraid or terrified because of them, for the Lord your God goes with you; he will never leave you nor forsake you.

John 8:44   You belong to your father, the devil, and you want to carry out your father's desire. He was a murderer from the beginning, not holding to the truth, for there is no truth in him. When he lies, he speaks his native language, for he is a liar and the father of lies.

Psalm 147:3 He heals the brokenhearted and binds up their wounds.

Matthew 2:18 A voice is heard in Ramah, weeping and great mourning, Rachel weeping for her children and refusing to be comforted, because they are no more.

2 Chronicles 30:9 If you return to the Lord, then your brothers and your children will be shown compassion by their captors and will come back to this land, for the Lord your God is gracious and compassionate. He will not turn his face from you if you to return to him.

Psalm 139:13-16 For you created my inmost being; you knit me together in my mother's womb. I praise you because I am fearfully and wonderfully made; your works are wonderful, I know that full well. My frame was not hidden from you when I was made in the secret place. When I was woven together in the depths of the earth, your eyes saw my unformed body. All the days ordained for me were written in your book before one of them came to be.

Jeremiah 31:3 The Lord appeared to us in the past, saying, "I have loved you with an everlasting love; I have drawn you with loving-kindness."

Revelation 21:4 He will wipe every tear from their eyes. There will be no more death or mourning or crying or pain, for the old order of things has passed away.

Matthew 7:2 For in the same way you judge others, you will be judged, and with the measure you use, it will be measured to you.

Psalm 98:8-9 Let the rivers clap their hands, let the mountains sing together for joy; let them sing before the Lord, for he comes to judge the earth. He will judge the world in righteousness and the peoples with equity.

Psalm 103:12 As far as the east is from the west, so far has he removed our transgressions from us.

Luke 23:34 Jesus said, "Father, forgive them, for they do not know what they are doing."

I John 2:2 He is the atoning sacrifice for our sins, and not only ours but also for the sins of the whole world.

1 Corinthians 6:20 You were bought with a price. Therefore, honor God with your body.

2 Corinthians 3:17 Now the Lord is the Spirit, and where the Spirit of the Lord is, there is freedom.

John 8:36 So if the Son sets you free, you will be free indeed.

Special Thanks

Thank you to my friends and family members who believed with me that God wanted me to write this book, and who encouraged me at various stages throughout this long process to keep it moving forward.

A special thanks to Sue, my mentor and friend from the Cleveland Pregnancy Center, for her review and valuable comments on the content of this book.

Thanks to Ben Barnhart for his editing skills, expertise and guidance, and for recognizing God's purpose for this book.

Thanks to Bethany for her help with aligning Scripture verses, and for her enthusiastic encouragement, which got this project going again.

Thank you to graphic artist Angela Hammersmith of Hammersmith Designs, who designed the cover, capturing my desire for simplicity.

Thank you to my sister Sheri for her loving encouragement and for her many hours of proofreading.

And special thanks to my daughter Julie for reading the initial manuscript with her heart, not just her eyes, her response so deeply touching my heart.

Thank you, God, for showing me my life's purpose. Use this book for your kingdom, Lord.

About the Author

Carol Jackson is a retired commercial property manager who lives near Cleveland, Ohio with her husband of twenty-five years. She is the mother of six children, grandma of ten, and recently welcomed her first great-grandson to the family.

She enjoys spending quality time with family and friends, traveling to new places (especially Israel), and volunteering at her church, Vineyard Cleveland.

If God spoke to you through this book, you are welcome to contact her at cjcreated2worship@gmail.com.

All proceeds from the sale of this book are to benefit:
The Cleveland Pregnancy Center

Heartbeat International

The National Memorial for the Unborn

Made in the USA
Coppell, TX
20 April 2021

54158360R10059